D1468139

REMARKABLE CANADIANS

Tommy Douglas

by Bryan Pezzi

Published by Weigl Educational Publishers Limited
6325 – 10 Street SE
Calgary, Alberta, Canada
T2H 2Z9

Website: www.weigl.com
Copyright ©2008 WEIGL EDUCATIONAL PUBLISHERS LIMITED

All of the Internet URLs given in the book were valid at the time of publication.
However, due to the dynamic nature of the Internet, some addresses may have changed,
or sites may have ceased to exist since publication. While the author and publisher
regret any inconvenience this may cause readers, no responsibility for any such changes
can be accepted by either the author or the publisher.

Library and Archives Canada Cataloguing in Publication

Pezzi, Bryan
    Tommy Douglas / Bryan Pezzi.

(Remarkable Canadians)
ISBN 978-1-55388-321-0 (bound)
ISBN 978-1-55388-322-7 (pbk.)
    1. Douglas, T. C. (Thomas Clement), 1904-1986--Juvenile literature.
2. Saskatchewan--Politics and government--1944-1964--Juvenile literature.
3. Prime ministers--Saskatchewan--Biography--Juvenile literature. 4. Social
reformers--Canada--Biography--Juvenile literature. I. Title. II. Series.

FC3525.1.D68P48 2007   j971.24'03092   C2006-906257-9

Printed in the United States of America
1 2 3 4 5 6 7 8 9 0 11 10 09 08 07

Editor: Liz Brown
Design: Terry Paulhus

We acknowledge the financial support of the Government of Canada through the Book
Publishing Industry Development Program (BPIDP) for our publishing activities.

Cover: Tommy Douglas was the premier of Saskatchewan from 1944 to 1961.

Photograph Credits
Cover: Douglas-Coldwell Foundation; Arnold Mckenzie: pages 5, 7 bottom, and 12;
Douglas-Coldwell Foundation: page 16; Glenbow Archives: pages 1 (NA-2864-
997a[per], 4 (NA-2864-997a[per], 13 top left (NA-2399-49), 14 (NA-1486-1), 18
(NA-2864-997j[per]; Manitoba Archives: page 15 (Foote Collection, Negative 2762);
Reprinted with permission from the Office of Protocol and Honours, Government
of Saskatchewan: page 7 top left and top right.

Every reasonable effort has been made to trace ownership and to obtain permission
to reprint copyright material. The publishers would be pleased to have any errors
or omissions brought to their attention so that they may be corrected in
subsequent printings.

Contents

Who Is Tommy Douglas?

Tommy Douglas was a **minister** and a **politician**. He lived in Weyburn, Saskatchewan, in the 1930s. During this time, many people living on the Prairies were very poor. Tommy wanted to help. He had many ideas about how the government could improve people's lives. Tommy thought that the government should help people who were sick or poor. He was a good speaker. He told the people in Weyburn about his ideas. The people elected Tommy to represent them in the **federal** government in Ottawa. In 1944, he became the **premier** of Saskatchewan and made many laws to improve people's lives.

"My friends, watch out for the little fellow with an idea."

Growing Up

Thomas Clement Douglas was born in 1904 in Falkirk, Scotland. Everybody called him Tommy. His parents, Tom and Anne, moved their family to Canada in 1910. They settled in Winnipeg, Manitoba. Family, work, and church were the most important things in Tommy's life.

The Douglases were poor. Sometimes, Tommy and his two younger sisters could not attend school. They had to work to earn money for their family. Tommy had many jobs. He worked in a whisky factory, had a paper route, and **apprenticed** in a printer's shop.

Although he worked hard, Tommy found ways to have fun. His family noticed that he had a talent for speaking and acting. At family gatherings, Tommy made speeches and repeated poems from memory. Sometimes, he acted in a local theatre.

In the early 1900s, many people moved to Winnipeg looking for jobs and land.

Saskatchewan Tidbits

COAT OF ARMS

TREE
White Birch

FLOWER
Western Red Lily

Saskatchewan's provincial bird is the sharp-tailed grouse.

Saskatchewan joined **Confederation** in 1905.

Saskatchewan produces more wheat than any other province. The province is sometimes called "Canada's bread basket."

Regina is the provincial capital of Saskatchewan.

About one million people live in Saskatchewan.

Think about it!

Saskatchewan is where Tommy began his political career. Research life in Saskatchewan during the 1930s. How do you think this lifestyle might have influenced Tommy's ideas and beliefs?

Practice Makes Perfect

Church, work, and studying were important parts of Tommy's life. Tommy studied public speaking. When he was not working or studying, he practised boxing. Tommy started boxing when he was 15 years of age.

When he was a young man, Tommy began volunteering at the Baptist church he attended. The Baptist Church is a type of Christian religion. Tommy enjoyed working at the church. He decided to attend university to become a minister.

Tommy won Manitoba's lightweight boxing championship twice.

In 1924, Tommy enrolled at Brandon College, a school run by the Baptist Church. Here, he took lessons to improve his speaking. Tommy also took part in drama, debating, and sports. At school, Tommy learned many important ideas about religion and politics. In 1931, Tommy became a Baptist minister. In 1934, Tommy earned a Master's of Arts degree in sociology from McMaster University in Hamilton, Ontario. Sociology is the study of human society.

QUICK FACTS

- Tommy married Irma Dempsey in 1930.

- Tommy and Irma's daughter is actress Shirley Douglas. Actor Kiefer Sutherland is Tommy's grandson.

- Tommy met Stanley Knowles at McMaster University. Knowles was also a politician. He helped start the Canada **Pension** Plan.

Tommy's grandson, Kiefer Sutherland, has a leading role in the television show *24*.

Key Events

Tommy moved to Weyburn for his first job as a minister. The 1930s were difficult years for people living on the Prairies. A **drought** caused many farmers' crops to fail, and most people lost their jobs because of the **Great Depression**. Tommy wanted to help people in his community. He thought that if he was elected to government he could improve people's lives.

In 1935, Tommy **campaigned** to represent the people of Weyburn in Canada's federal government. He won the **election** and travelled to Ottawa to begin his job as a **member of parliament**.

Tommy spent nine years in Ottawa as a member of parliament. In 1944, Tommy campaigned to become the premier of Saskatchewan and won the election. As head of the provincial government, Tommy could do more to help the people of Saskatchewan.

Tommy was elected premier of Saskatchewan five times between 1944 and 1960.

Thoughts from Tommy

Tommy gave many speeches as a politician and minister. Here are some of the things he has said.

Tommy works as a church minister during the Great Depression. He sees many people suffer.

"How do you talk to a man about saving his soul if he's got a toothache?"

Tommy tries to inspire people to work for the benefit of others.

"Measure your life, not by what you get, but by what you give."

As premier of Saskatchewan, Tommy introduces a new health plan.

"People should be able to get whatever health services they require irrespective of their individual capacity to pay."

Tommy talks about the importance of dreaming.

"Where people have no dreams...life becomes dull and a meaningless wilderness."

Tommy wants to become a politician so he can help people.

"I'm not interested in getting power unless you can do something with this power."

Tommy is a good public speaker. People enjoy his charm and humour.

"One of the things I tried to do when I was in politics...was to try and retain my sense of humour."

What Is a Premier?

Tommy was the premier of Saskatchewan. A premier is the head of the government in a Canadian province or territory.

Each province or territory has a **legislature** where laws are made. Usually, the premier is the leader of the political party with the most members in the legislature.

The premier appoints other people in his or her **political party** to the **cabinet**. People in the cabinet are called ministers. The premier and the ministers propose new laws to other members of the legislature. Everyone in the legislature votes to decide if these laws should become official.

🍁 The Saskatchewan cabinet meets in the Saskatchewan legislative building. The building was built between 1908 and 1912.

Premiers 101

William Aberhart (1878–1943)

Premier of Alberta, 1935–1943

Achievements: Like Tommy Douglas, William Aberhart was a preacher and politician during the Great Depression. People called him "Bible Bill" because he preached on a Christian radio program. Aberhart started a political party called Social Credit. He believed that the government should give people money to help them live better lives.

Joseph Smallwood (1900–1991)

Premier of Newfoundland and Labrador, 1949–1972

Achievements: Joseph Smallwood was Newfoundland and Labrador's first premier. Newfoundland and Labrador was once a colony of Great Britain. In 1946, Smallwood was chosen to lead a group to decide the future of the colony. The people in the colony had three choices—they could remain a colony, become a country, or join Canada. Smallwood wanted Newfoundland and Labrador to join Canada. In 1949, the people of Newfoundland and Labrador voted to join Canada. Smallwood became premier of the province.

René Lévesque (1922–1987)

Premier of Quebec, 1976–1985

Achievements: René Lévesque was a Quebec journalist who was interested in politics. In 1968, he founded a new party called the Parti Québécois. Lévesque wanted Quebec to separate from Canada and become its own country. His party won Quebec's 1976 election. Lévesque was premier of Quebec until 1985.

Paul Okalik (1964–)

Premier of Nunavut, 1999

Achievements: Paul Okalik is Nunavut's first premier. Nunavut is Canada's third territory. Okalik worked for many years to help make Nunavut a territory. He has helped create the Nunavut Wildlife Management Board and the Inuit Heritage Trust. Okalik was elected to the territory's first government in 1999 and has been premier ever since.

Provincial Elections

Members of a provincial government are chosen in an election. A provincial election must be held at least once every five years. The premier decides when to call an election. Candidates compete for a seat in the legislature. Most candidates represent a political party. On election day, people vote for a candidate to represent their area. The party that wins the most seats forms the government. The leader of that party becomes the premier. The premier must win a seat in the legislature to lead his or her party in government.

Influences

Tommy was influenced by several people. He learned many of his beliefs from his family. Tommy's family believed that workers should be treated fairly by their bosses and have more power in their jobs. His family discussed these ideas in their home. They were strong supporters of the labour movement. This was a political idea to protect the rights of workers.

When Tommy was young, his minister at church influenced his ideas about workers' rights. The minister's name was J.S. Woodsworth. Woodsworth taught Tommy about the "social gospel." This was the belief that people should help others who were poor and sick.

🍁 J.S. Woodsworth became the first leader of the national Co-operative Commonwealth Federation (CCF) in 1933. The CCF was a political party that supported the labour movement.

Certain events influenced Tommy's decision to help people. When Tommy was 14 years old, thousands of people in Winnipeg stopped working to **protest** poor wages and working conditions. This protest was called the Winnipeg General **Strike**. One day, Tommy was working on his newspaper route when he saw the Royal Canadian Mounted Police shoot guns at a crowd of protesting workers. They killed two men and arrested J.S. Woodsworth. This day became known as "Bloody Saturday." Seeing these events made Tommy want to help workers.

THE WINNIPEG GENERAL STRIKE

The Winnipeg General Strike stopped business in Winnipeg in 1919 for more than one month. Thirty-thousand people stopped going to their jobs. They wanted better wages and improved working conditions. Businesses were forced to close. Government services could not operate. Workers returned to work after "Bloody Saturday." They feared that more people would be hurt if they did not stop protesting.

🍁 The Winnipeg General Strike began on May 15, 1919, at 11 a.m.

Overcoming Obstacles

Tommy was very sick when he was young. There was a bone infection in his leg that needed many operations. None of the operations helped him. Tommy's family could not afford to send him to a special doctor.

When Tommy was 10, his doctor said he needed to remove Tommy's leg to stop the infection from spreading to the rest of his body. A visiting **surgeon** operated on Tommy for free. This meant that Tommy did not lose his leg. The experience taught Tommy about the importance of doctors. He wanted everyone to receive the medical care they needed, even if they did not have a great deal of money.

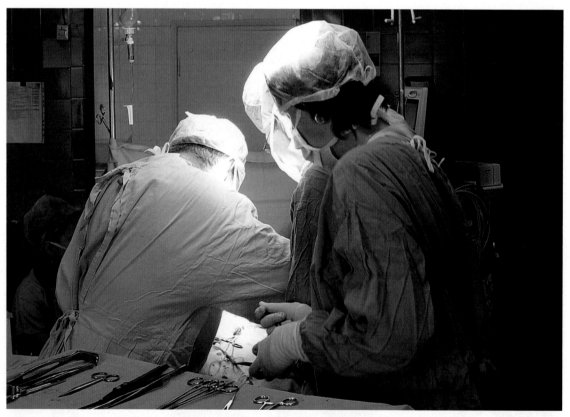

In 1947, Tommy created the Universal Hospital Services plan. This plan ensured that everyone in Saskatchewan would be able to have treatment at a hospital if they needed it.

As a politician, Tommy worked hard to make health care available to all Canadians at no cost. In 1962, he introduced a system called Medicare. Under this system, all Canadians receive medical care when they need it. All Canadians share the cost of this care through taxes.

Many doctors opposed this plan. They did not want to depend on the government to be paid. Even though the doctors did not want Medicare, Saskatchewan's government began offering it to the people. Soon, Medicare began to be used in other provinces.

🍁 Today, Tommy is known as the "Father of Medicare."

Achievements and Successes

Tommy had a long career as a politician. He was premier of Saskatchewan from 1944 to 1961. Tommy's political party, called the CCF, supported socialism. Socialism is a system in which the government manages the economy, health care, and other services.

Tommy ran the first socialist government in North America. During his 17 years as premier, he introduced many new social programs in Saskatchewan. Many of these programs were later copied in other parts of Canada.

Tommy was known as a good speaker. He would tell many jokes in his speeches.

After Tommy resigned as premier in 1961, he became the leader of the New Democratic Party (NDP) in the federal government. The NDP was the new name of the CCF party. Tommy worked in the House of Commons until his retirement in 1979. In 1981, he became a Companion of the Order of Canada. This award is given to Canadians who have worked hard to improve the country. It is one of Canada's highest awards.

Tommy died in 1986. Years after his death, Canadians still celebrate the life of Tommy Douglas. In 2004, Tommy was named the greatest Canadian of all time in a poll by the Canadian Broadcasting Corporation (CBC) television network.

THE CCF AND THE NDP

The Co-operative Commonwealth Federation was founded in 1932. The people who began this political party wanted a society where everyone would help each other for the common good. The CCF wanted more social programs, such as Medicare, old age pensions, and family allowances. These programs provide money for senior citizens and people who have children.

The CCF later became the NDP. The NDP has formed governments in Saskatchewan, British Columbia, Manitoba, Ontario, and the Yukon.

🍁 Jack Layton was elected leader of the federal NDP in 2003.

Write a Biography

A person's life story can be the subject of a book. This kind of book is called a biography. Biographies describe the lives of remarkable people, such as those who have achieved great success or have done important things to help others. These people may be alive today, or they may have lived many years ago. Reading a biography can help you learn more about a remarkable person.

At school, you might be asked to write a biography. First, decide who you want to write about. You can choose a politician, such as Tommy Douglas, or any other person you find interesting. Then, find out if your library has any books about this person. Learn as much as you can about him or her. Write down the key events in this person's life. What was this person's childhood like? What has he or she accomplished? What are his or her goals? What makes this person special or unusual?

A concept web is a useful research tool. Read the questions in the following concept web. Answer the questions in your notebook. Your answers will help you write your biography.

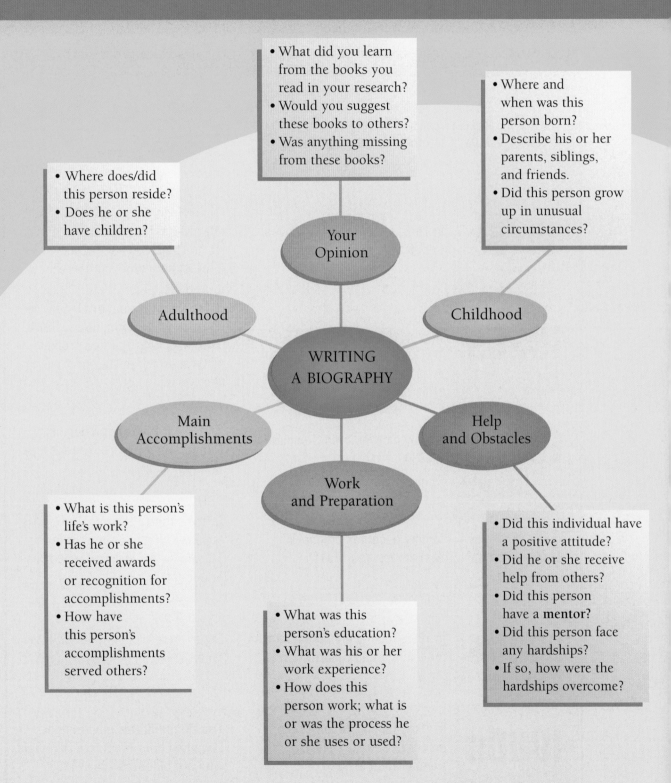

- What did you learn from the books you read in your research?
- Would you suggest these books to others?
- Was anything missing from these books?

- Where and when was this person born?
- Describe his or her parents, siblings, and friends.
- Did this person grow up in unusual circumstances?

- Where does/did this person reside?
- Does he or she have children?

Your Opinion

Adulthood

Childhood

WRITING A BIOGRAPHY

Main Accomplishments

Help and Obstacles

Work and Preparation

- What is this person's life's work?
- Has he or she received awards or recognition for accomplishments?
- How have this person's accomplishments served others?

- Did this individual have a positive attitude?
- Did he or she receive help from others?
- Did this person have a **mentor**?
- Did this person face any hardships?
- If so, how were the hardships overcome?

- What was this person's education?
- What was his or her work experience?
- How does this person work; what is or was the process he or she uses or used?

Timeline

DECADE	TOMMY DOUGLAS	WORLD EVENTS
1900s	Tommy Douglas is born in Falkirk, Scotland, on October 20, 1904.	On January 22, 1905, workers protest the working conditions in St. Petersburg, Russia.
1910s	In 1910, Tommy's family moves from Scotland to Winnipeg.	The Winnipeg General Strike takes place from May 15 to June 25, 1919. Thousands of workers protest poor working conditions.
1920s	Tommy enrols in Brandon College in 1924.	Vladimir Lenin, leader of the Russian **Revolution**, dies in 1924. The revolution sparked protests for workers' rights around the world.
1930s	Tommy marries Irma Dempsey in 1930.	The Great Depression begins. Canadians suffer from poor crops and high unemployment.
1940s	Tommy becomes premier of Saskatchewan in 1944.	In 1947, the Taft-Hartley Labor Act is passed in the United States. This limits the ability of workers to go on strike.
1950s	In 1959, Tommy announces a plan for Medicare in Saskatchewan.	Steelworkers in the United States go on strike for 116 days in 1959.
1960s	In 1961, Tommy becomes the leader of Canada's New Democratic Party.	The United States government begins to offer Medicare to people who are older than 65 in 1965.

Further Research

How can I find out more about Tommy Douglas?

Most libraries have computers that connect to a database for researching information. If you input a key word, you will be provided with a list of books in the library that contain information on that topic. Non-fiction books are arranged numerically, using their call number. Fiction books are organized alphabetically by the author's last name.

Websites

To find out more about Tommy Douglas, go to www.tommydouglas.ca/tommy/life

To watch video news clips and interviews with Tommy Douglas, go to http://archives.cbc.ca and type, "Tommy Douglas" into the archives search engine.

Words to Know

apprenticed: learned a trade

cabinet: a group of lawmakers made up of the premier and his government ministers

campaigned: gathered support

Confederation: the creation of Canada in 1867

drought: a shortage of water caused by no rain falling for many days

election: the process of voting people into power

federal: a level of government that includes all of Canada

Great Depression: a time between 1930 and 1940 when the economy was weak and people could not find jobs

legislature: the place where provincial laws are passed, also called the legislative assembly

member of parliament: a person elected to represent his or her community in the federal government

mentor: a wise and trusted teacher

minister: the leader of a church

pension: money given to a person when he or she retires

political party: group of people who share similar views on how the government should work

politician: a person who is elected to work in the government

premier: the head of government in a province

protest: taking part in speeches and actions to object something

revolution: a major change in government or society

strike: stopping work as an objection to something

surgeon: a doctor who performs operations

Index